Out of Sight
Pictures of Hidden Worlds

Seymour Simon

SEASTAR BOOKS

NEW YORK

This book is gratefully dedicated to David Reuther, my longtime friend and editor.

Page 1: The head of a bedbug, magnified about 26X in this scanning electron micrograph (SEM). This page: An SEM of a blood clot, magnified about 6,000X. A computer was used to color the thin, yellowish strands of fibrin, a clotting material in blood. Page 48: Two grains of pollen on a sunflower petal, magnified about 1,600X in this SEM.

Permission to use the following photographs is gratefully acknowledged:
Andrew Davidhazy/RIT: pages 31, 32, 33, 34, 35; NASA: pages 40, 41, 44, 45; B. Balick (University of Washington)/NASA: pages 46–47; J. Hester and P. Scowen (Arizona State University)/NASA: pages 42–43; Ulrich Buettner/Nikon: pages 4-5; NOAA: page 37; James Hayden/Phototake: pages 6–7; Dr. Dennis Kunkel/Phototake: pages 1, 10–11, 15, 16–17, 29, 48; Aeroservice/Photo Researchers, Inc.: page 38; Dr. Jeremy Burgess/Photo Researchers, Inc.: page 13; Patrice Loiez Cern/Photo Researchers, Inc.: pages 18–19; Clinique Ste Catherine/CNRI/Photo Researchers, Inc.: page 23; CNRI/Photo Researchers, Inc.: page 12; Earth Satellite Corporation/Photo Researchers, Inc.: page 39; Cecil Fox/Photo Researchers, Inc.: page 28; GJLP/CNRI/Photo Researchers, Inc.: page 24; Mehau Kulyk/Photo Researchers, Inc.: pages 8–9, 25; Professor P. Motta/Department of Anatomy/University "La Sapienza," Rome/Photo Researchers, Inc.: pages 2–3; Quest/Photo Researchers, Inc.: page 14; Siu/Photo Researchers, Inc.: pages 20–21; stockphoto.com: front cover, pages 22, 26–27; Howard Sochurek Inc.: back cover.

Library of Congress Cataloging-in-Publication Data
Simon, Seymour. Out of sight: pictures of hidden worlds / Seymour Simon.   p. cm.
Summary: Shows pictures of objects which are too small, too far away, or too fast to see without mechanical assistance such as microscopes, telescopes, X-rays, and other techniques.   ISBN 1-58717-011-6 (trade bdg.) — ISBN 1-58717-012-4 (lib. bdg.)
1. Vision — Juvenile literature.   2. Microscopy — Juvenile literature.   3. Telescopes — Juvenile literature.   4. Radiography — Juvenile literature. [1. Vision. 2. Senses and sensation. 3. Microscopy. 4. Telescopes. 5. Radiography.] I. Title.
QP475.7 .S555 2000   612.8'4—dc21   00-025684

The text for this book is set in 16-point Garamond Book.

ISBN 1-58717-011-6 (trade edition)
1 3 5 7 9 HC 10 8 6 4 2
ISBN 1-58717-012-4 (library edition)
3 5 7 9 LE 10 8 6 4 2
ISBN 1-58717-149-X (paperback edition)
1 3 5 7 9 PB 10 8 6 4 2

PRINTED BY PROOST NV IN BELGIUM

For more information about our books, and the authors and artists who create them,
visit our web site: www.northsouth.com

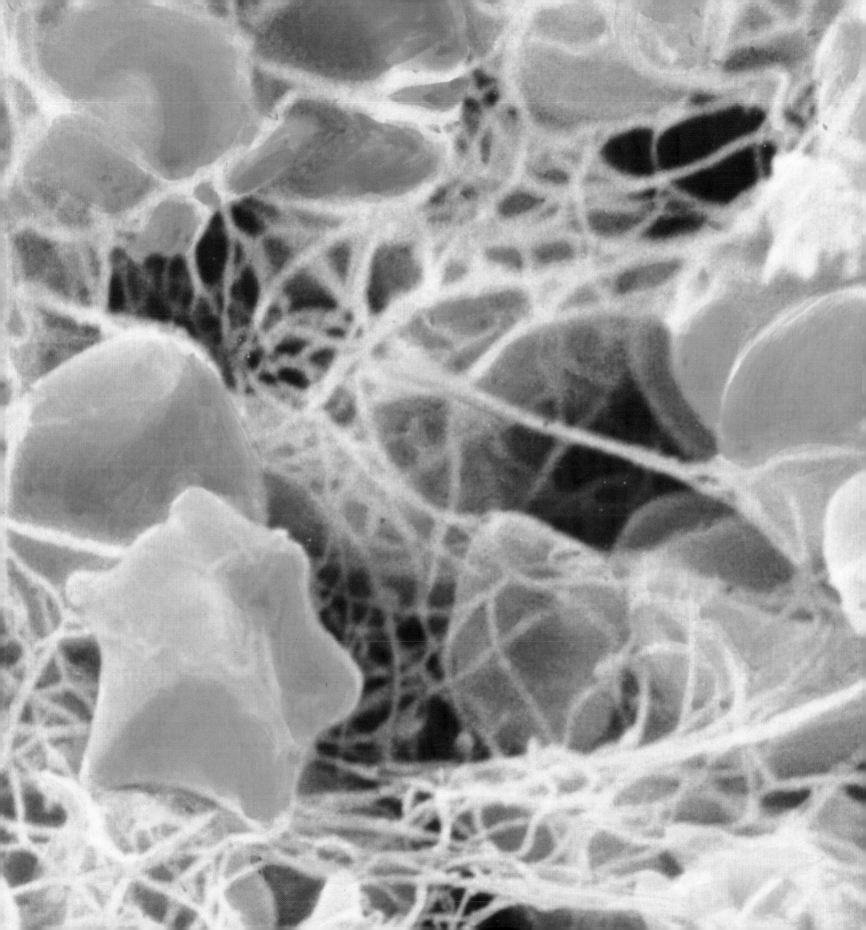

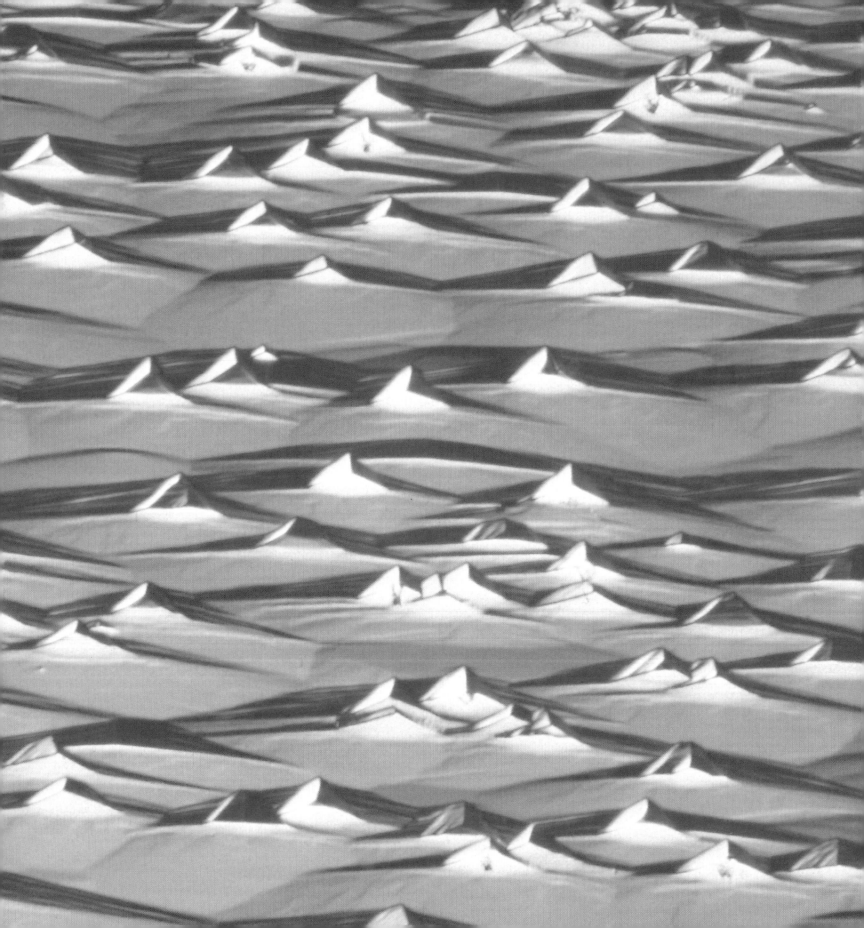

Introduction

You can see so many different things around you. You use your eyes to see a tiny insect, or a star billions of miles away, or a rocket thundering off a launch pad.

Yet all around you are countless sights that your eyes cannot see. There are worlds that are too small, too distant, too fast. There are worlds that are behind or within other objects. And there are kinds of light that your eyes just cannot see.

We first began to learn of the hidden worlds around us with the inventions of the telescope and microscope. Nearly four hundred years ago, Galileo turned a small telescope to the night sky and saw for the first time the moons of Jupiter and the rings of Saturn. Sixty-five years later, Leeuwenhoek used a simple microscope to view tiny animals swimming in a drop of water. Today, we have a whole variety of instruments that can view the inside of a human body, capture a bullet in flight, see the birth of stars in far-off space, and picture the inside of an atom.

This book explores some of the worlds around you that your eyes cannot see. We hope that you will enjoy this search for hidden worlds.

The surface of a crystal, magnified about 2,300X.

Hidden Worlds Around You

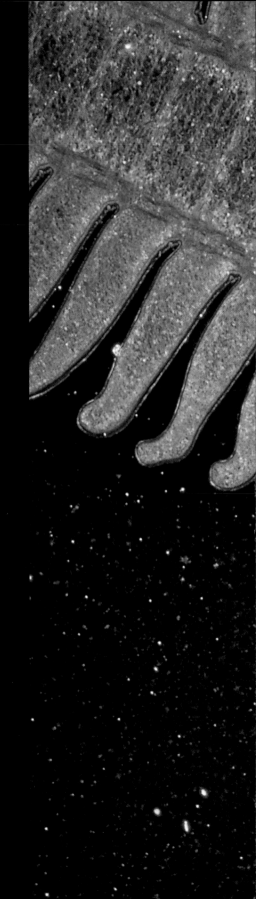

All around you are worlds too small to be seen with your unaided eye. In Holland in 1674, Anton van Leeuwenhoek used a single-lens microscope to enlarge the view of tiny objects. A single lens may magnify an object up to twenty times, which is usually written 20X. Two or more lenses are used in compound microscopes, which are more powerful. For example, if one lens magnifies 5X, and the other 20X, then the total magnification is 5 multiplied by 20, or 100X. Even a single magnifying lens can help you to begin exploring some hidden worlds on your own. For example, you can use a lens to examine an insect or a tiny water animal or plant.

This is a photomicrograph of the head of a tapeworm, magnified about 30X. A tapeworm is a flat worm that lives inside the digestive system of some animals, such as fishes, frogs, horses, or cows. Tapeworms are sometimes even found in people. Tapeworms can range in body length from about half an inch to thirty feet, but their heads are much smaller. This tapeworm was in the intestines of a horse. Its head has hooks that attach it to the host's intestine. A tapeworm has no mouth or digestive tract, so it absorbs food through its body surface.

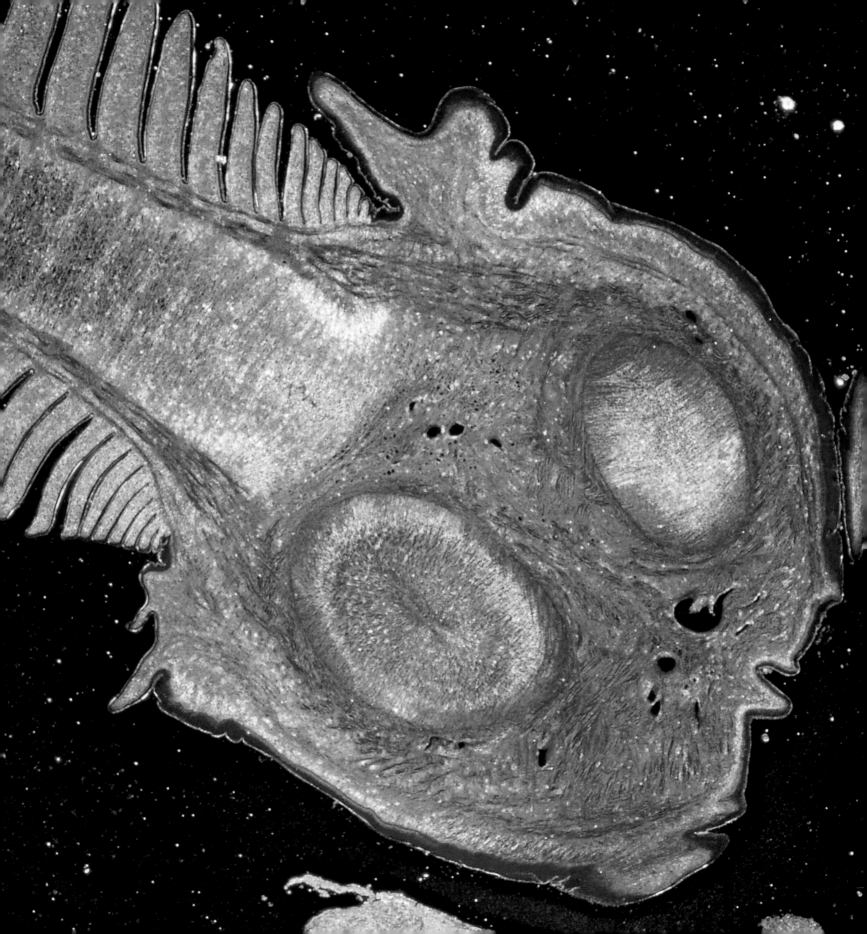

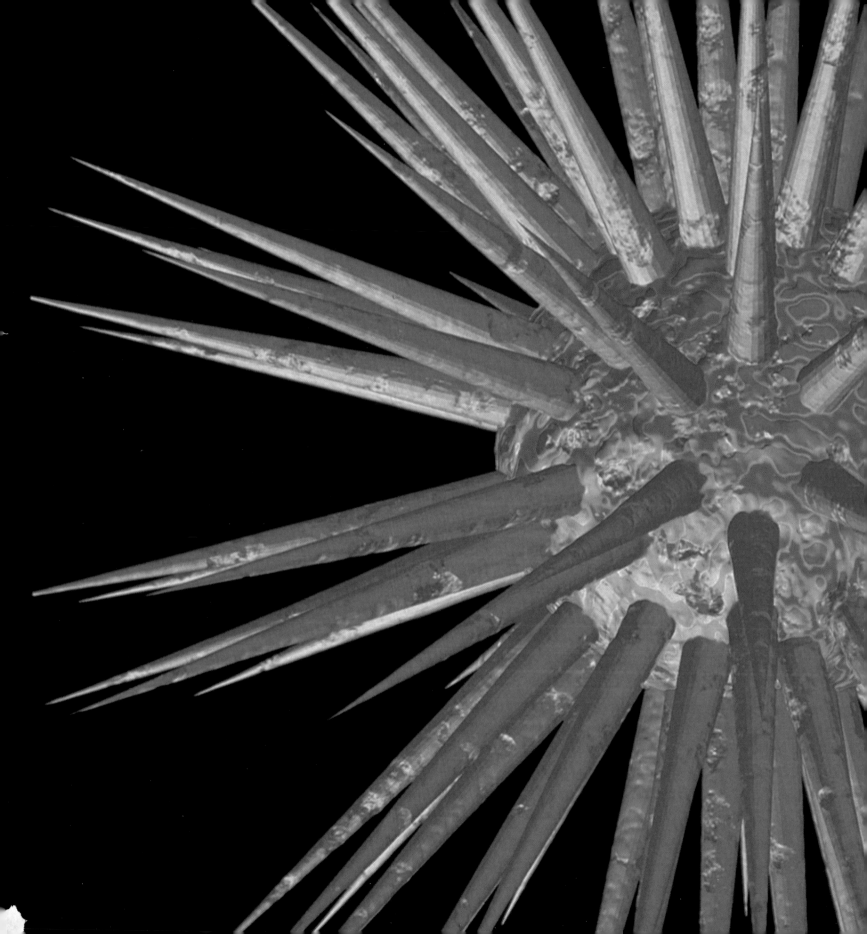

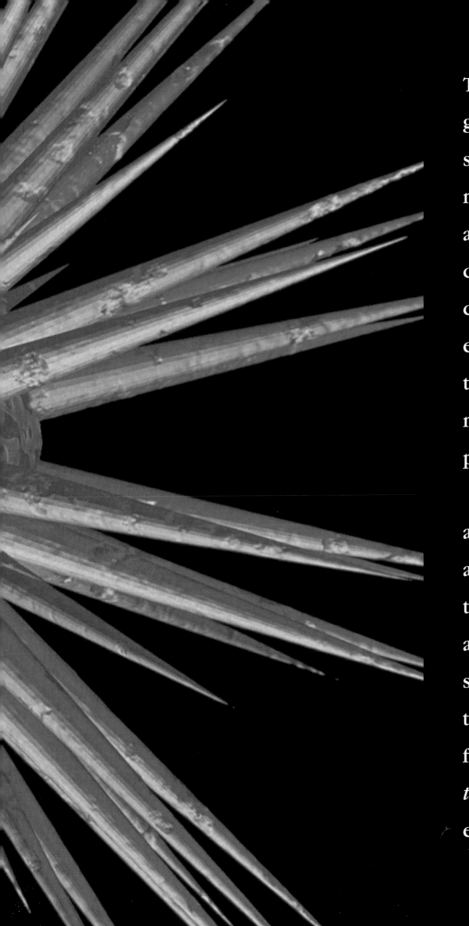

This "exploding star" is actually a computer-generated three-dimensional picture of a spiked virus as seen through an electron microscope. Viruses are found in humans, animals, plants, and even bacteria. They cause infections of various kinds, from colds and influenza to more serious diseases such as AIDS. Viruses are 20 to 100 times smaller than the smallest bacteria— much too small to be seen by even the most powerful microscope that uses light.

A light microscope can magnify up to about 1,200X. That means that an object about the thickness of a human hair or a thread can be magnified so that it looks like a tree trunk. Beyond 1,200X, light microscopes are not useful because they lose details. Electron microscopes use magnetic fields as lenses to capture objects 10 to 100 *thousand* times smaller than the human eye can see.

This colorful-looking monster is actually the head of a ladybug, magnified about 57X. The image is called an SEM, or scanning electron micrograph. The SEM is a special kind of electron microscope. An SEM user can look over a specimen from different angles, zoom in and out, and select a particular view. Then he or she just presses a button to photograph what is seen.

Ladybugs have small heads, and bodies about half an inch long. They are often colored red or orange with spots of white, yellow, or black. They don't have the colors seen in this image. A computer processed the SEM and put in the colors to make the details easier to see.

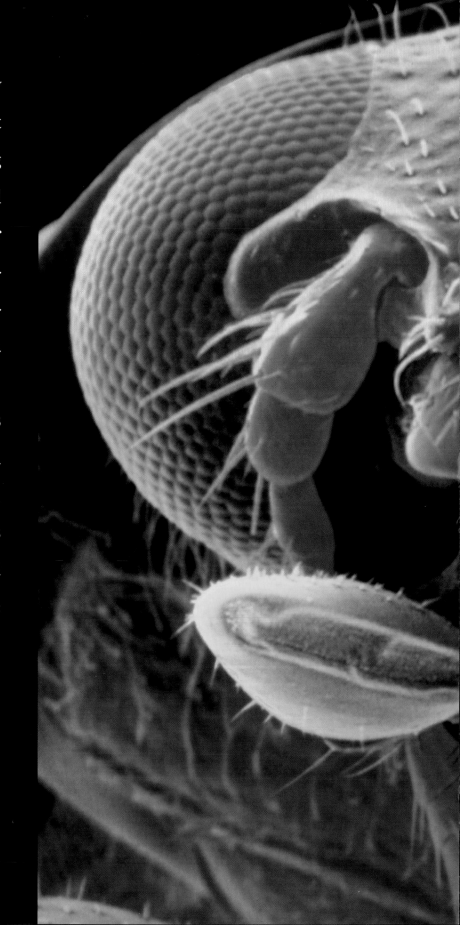

This is not a green monster from Mars. It is an SEM of a head louse on a strand of human hair, magnified about 320X. A head louse is a flat, wingless insect one-tenth of an inch long, about the size of a pinhead. It has a claw at the end of each leg that helps it hold on to the hair. The head louse, along with several other kinds of lice, lives on the blood of its host.

Can you imagine what this is? It's Velcro—a fastening tape sometimes used with clothing and shoes. The magnification of this SEM is about 140X. One piece of the fastening tape is covered with many tiny hooks; the other piece is covered with many tiny loops. Pressing the strips of material together ensures that many of the hooks go through the loops and keep a sneaker closed.

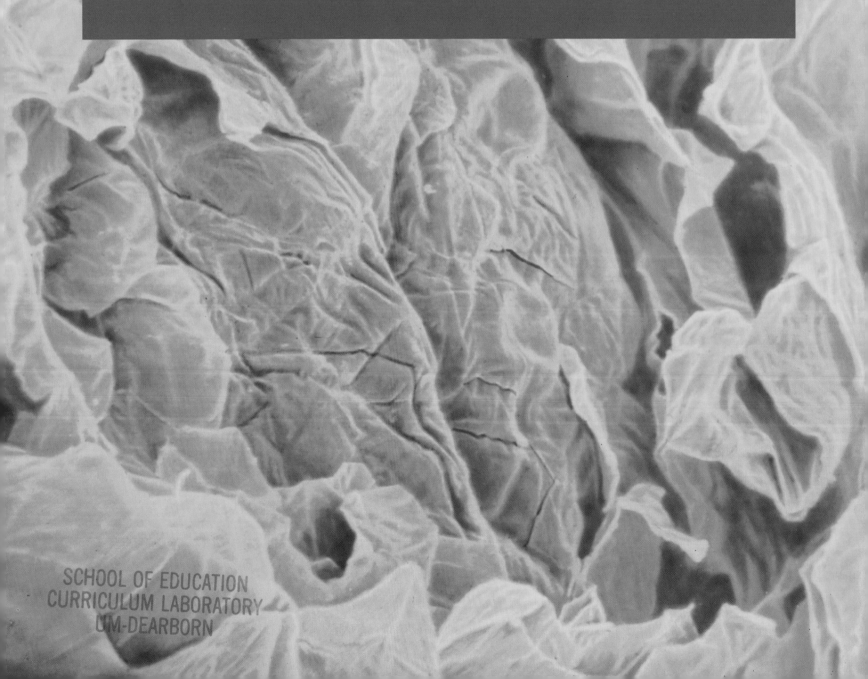

This is a computer-colored SEM of the surface of healthy human skin, magnified about 500X. Rough flakes of dead skin are being shed from the epidermis, the outside layer of the skin. One square inch of skin can contain up to fifteen feet of blood vessels and hundreds of sweat glands. The blood vessels and the sweat glands help to regulate the body's temperature.

See what happens when you don't brush your teeth? This is an SEM of the surface of a tooth, magnified about 2,700X. Plaque, the orange substance in this photo, and tartar, shown in yellow, are mineral substances that build up on the surface of teeth. Brushing helps slow them down or prevents them from forming. Dentists remove both plaque and tartar when cleaning your teeth.

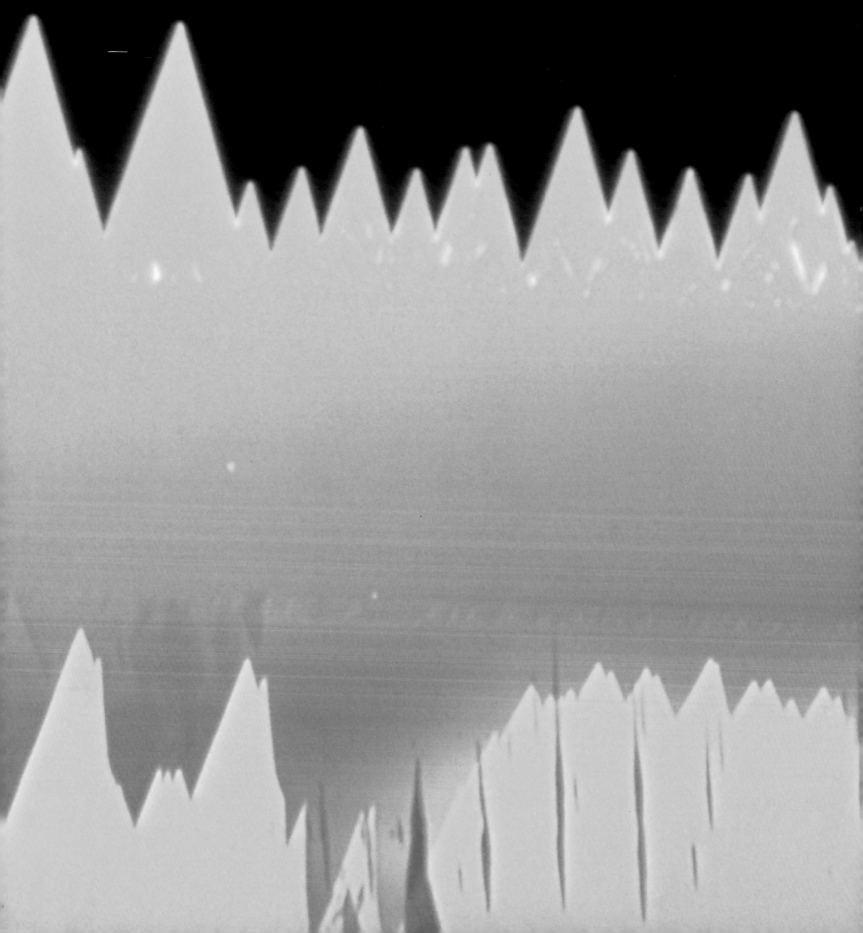

This photo looks like strange red and yellow mountains on some distant world in space. Actually, the photo was taken through a microscope with a magnification of about 360X. It shows a substance in the blood called cholesterol, a molecule found in animal fats and oils. The photo was made by using polarized light—light that passes through a special filter in only one plane, rather than in all directions.

These beautiful circles and spirals are the paths of sub-atomic particles millions of times smaller than the period at the end of this sentence. These high-energy particles are released by radioactive substances, such as uranium or plutonium. The particles are much too tiny and travel too quickly to be seen by even an electron microscope, so scientists use what's called a bubble chamber to "see" the paths the particles make as they move. This photograph was made at CERN, the European particle-physics laboratory at Geneva, Switzerland.

A bubble chamber contains a pure liquid material that is under pressure and heated beyond its boiling point. As a subatomic particle moves through the liq-uid, it leaves tiny bubbles in its wake, forming a visible line. The bubble paths are photographed and the sub-atomic particles that make them can be analyzed to find their electrical charge, energy, and how they interact with one another.

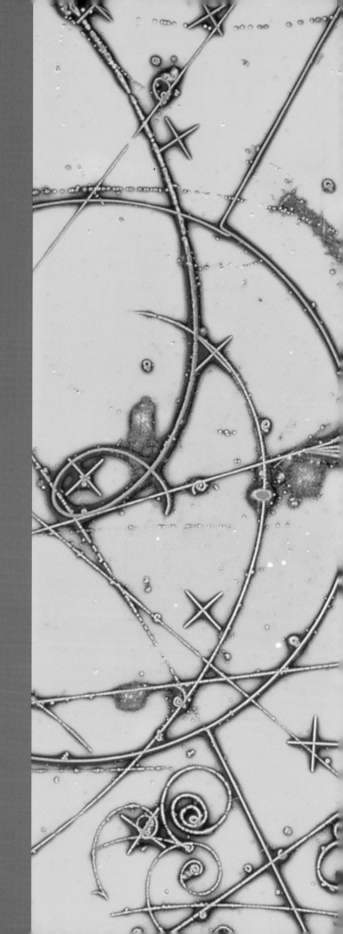

Hidden Worlds
Inside Your Body

What did early people know about the human body? They could easily see the skin, hair, fingers, and toes. They could listen to the beating of the heart, feel the movement of a muscle, or the hardness of a bone. But they knew very little about the inside of the body. Today, microscopes, X-ray machines, and many new inventions are giving us a detailed look at what's inside our bodies.

This photo of the inside of a living heart was taken with the aid of fiber optics and an instrument called an endoscope. Thousands of glass fibers, each about one-fifth the diameter of a human hair, are bundled together in a long, flexible tube half the thickness of a pencil. Two fiber-optic tubes are inserted into the body. Light travels down through one of the tubes, and the photograph is taken through the other.

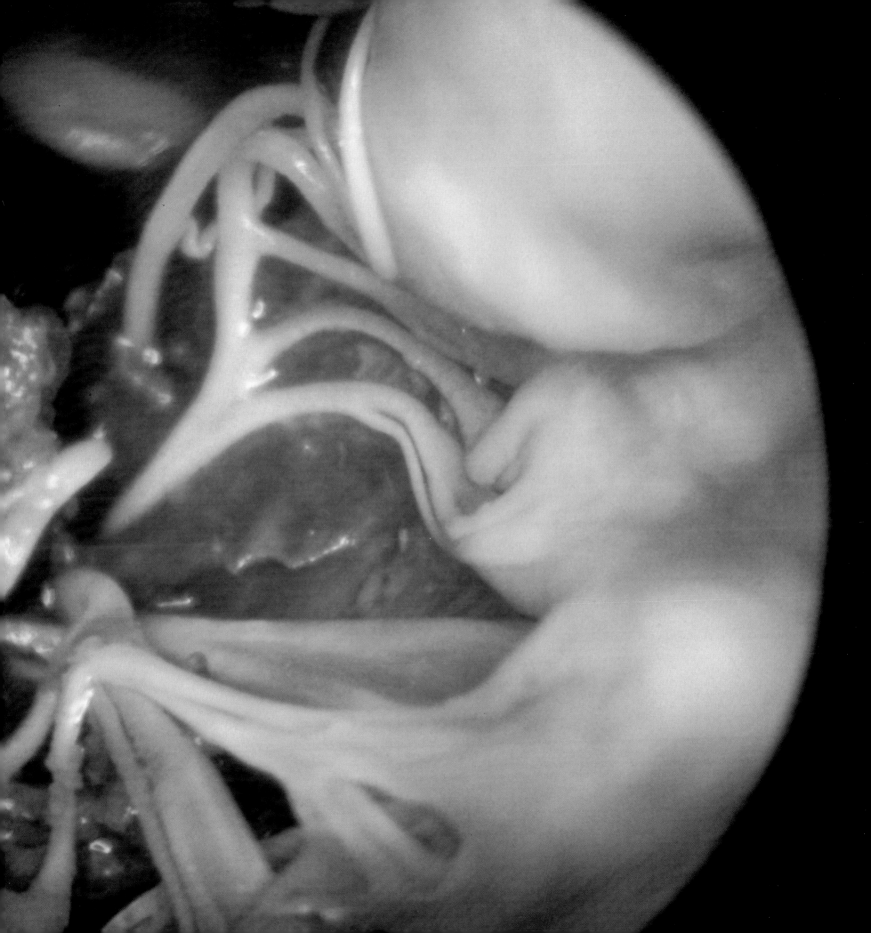

In this tomogram of a lung, low short-lasting doses of rays are sent through the body. The rays are set at different angles to avoid one organ getting in the way of another and causing unwanted shadows. The colors were added by a computer to make details easier to see.

This is a cross-sectional X ray through the abdomen of a living person. CAT scans (computerized axial tomography) are an important advance in the medical use of X rays. A thin, flat beam of X rays is sent through a person's body, and dozens of photographs are taken in a circle around the patient. A computer combines the results, making it possible to look at a slice of the body from any angle. In this CAT scan, the liver, at the left, is colored yellow, and the gall bladder is colored purple. The two kidneys, which are red, are at the bottom, separated by the spine.

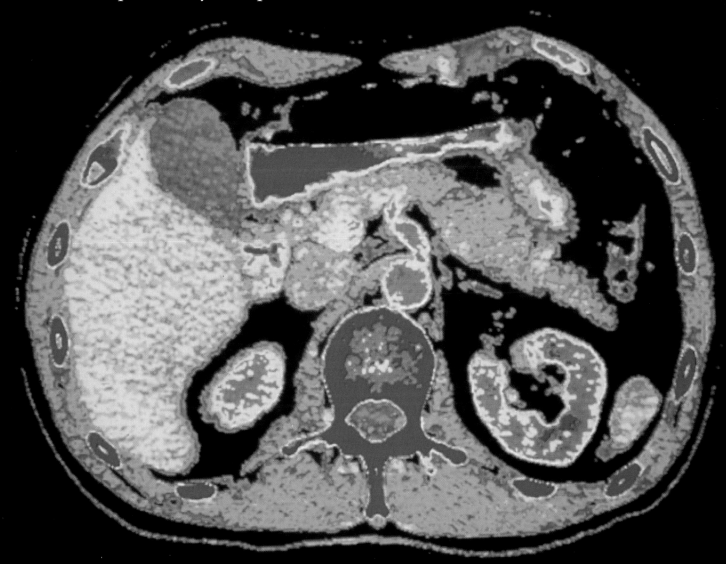

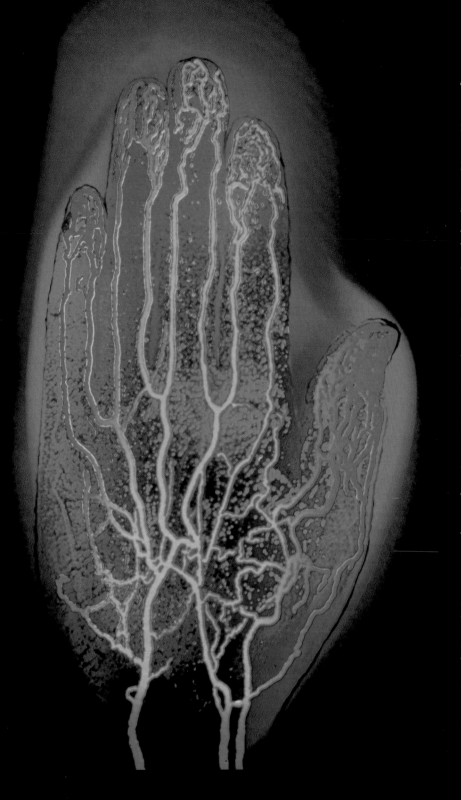

This is an arteriogram of a person's hand. The arteries are shown in orange. A dye is injected into blood vessels in the region where the picture is to be taken, and the subject is then X-rayed. The dye in the blood in the arteries blocks the X rays from passing through. The resulting X ray is colored by a computer to make the picture easier to see. On the opposite page is an MRI scan of a human head. It shows the brain, the airways, and the tongue. MRI stands for magnetic resonance imaging. To take an MRI, a person is placed within a very strong magnetic field, 30,000 times stronger than the earth's field. This makes the hydrogen atoms in the body line up temporarily in the same direction. When a pulse of radio waves is directed at the body, the atoms reflect the waves back to the scanner.

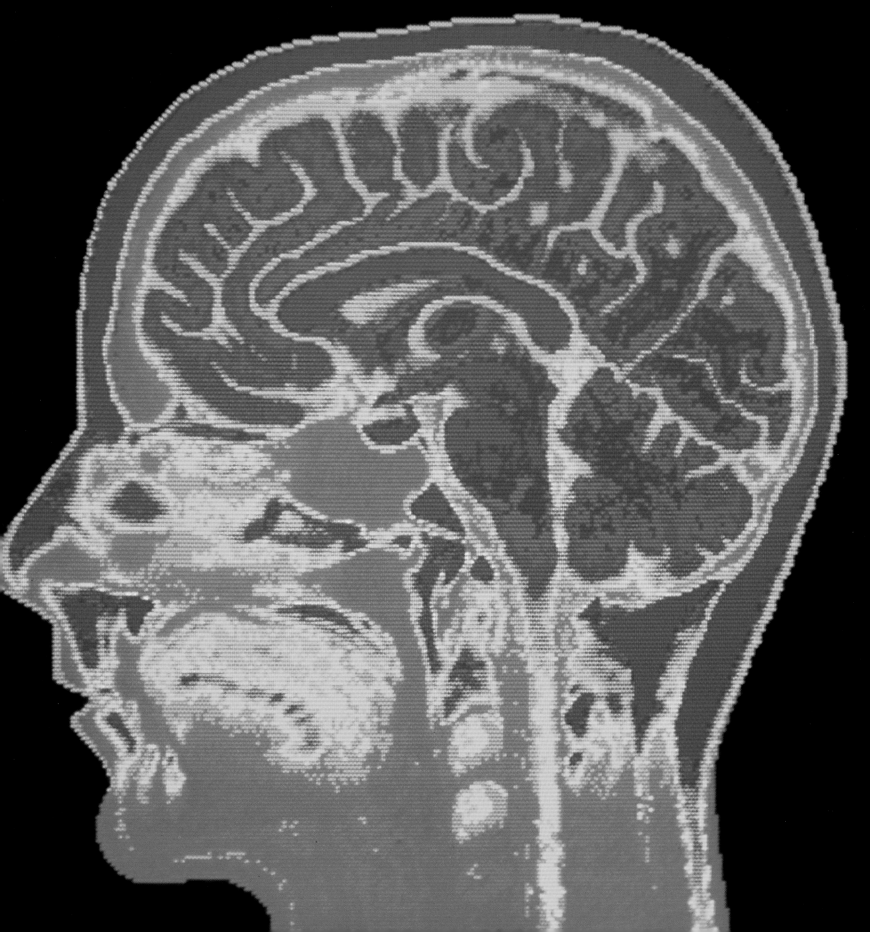

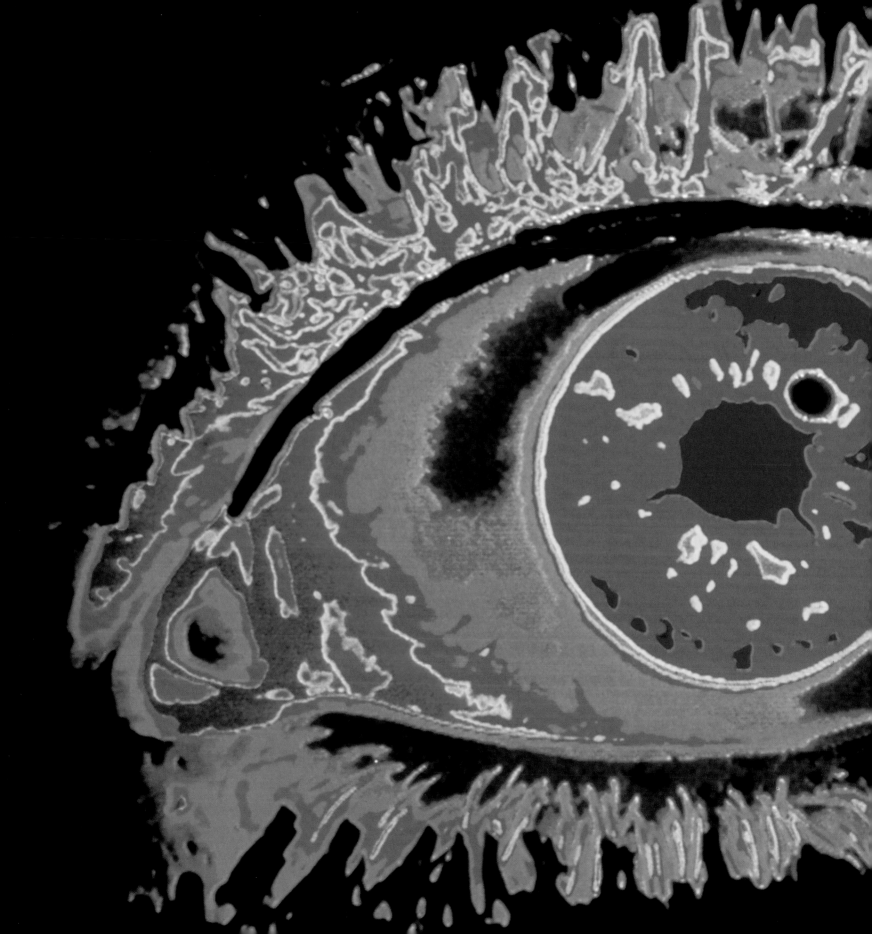

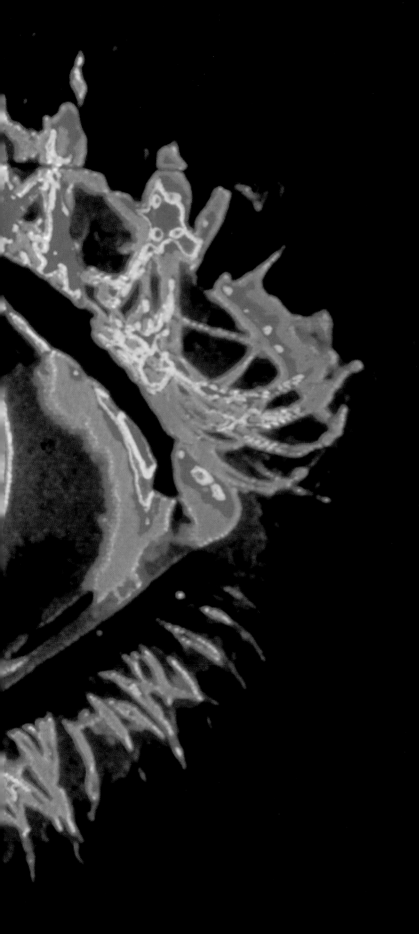

This unusual picture of an eye was made by using heat waves given off by the body. Called a thermogram, it uses a camera and film that is sensitive to infrared or heat rays. Differences in skin temperature depend upon the number of blood vessels and how close they are to the body's surface. A strange variation in a thermogram could be a sign that something is wrong. For example, an unusual warm spot might be the site of a cancer, and a cold spot might be the sign of a bloodstream blockage.

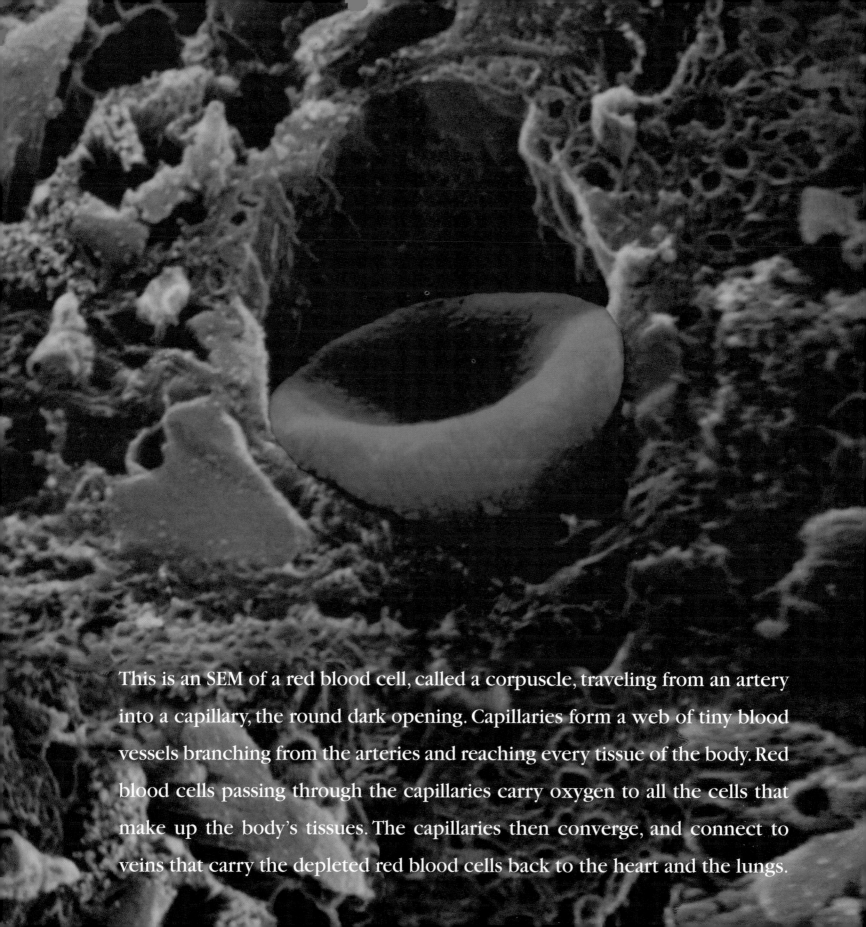

This is an SEM of a red blood cell, called a corpuscle, traveling from an artery into a capillary, the round dark opening. Capillaries form a web of tiny blood vessels branching from the arteries and reaching every tissue of the body. Red blood cells passing through the capillaries carry oxygen to all the cells that make up the body's tissues. The capillaries then converge, and connect to veins that carry the depleted red blood cells back to the heart and the lungs.

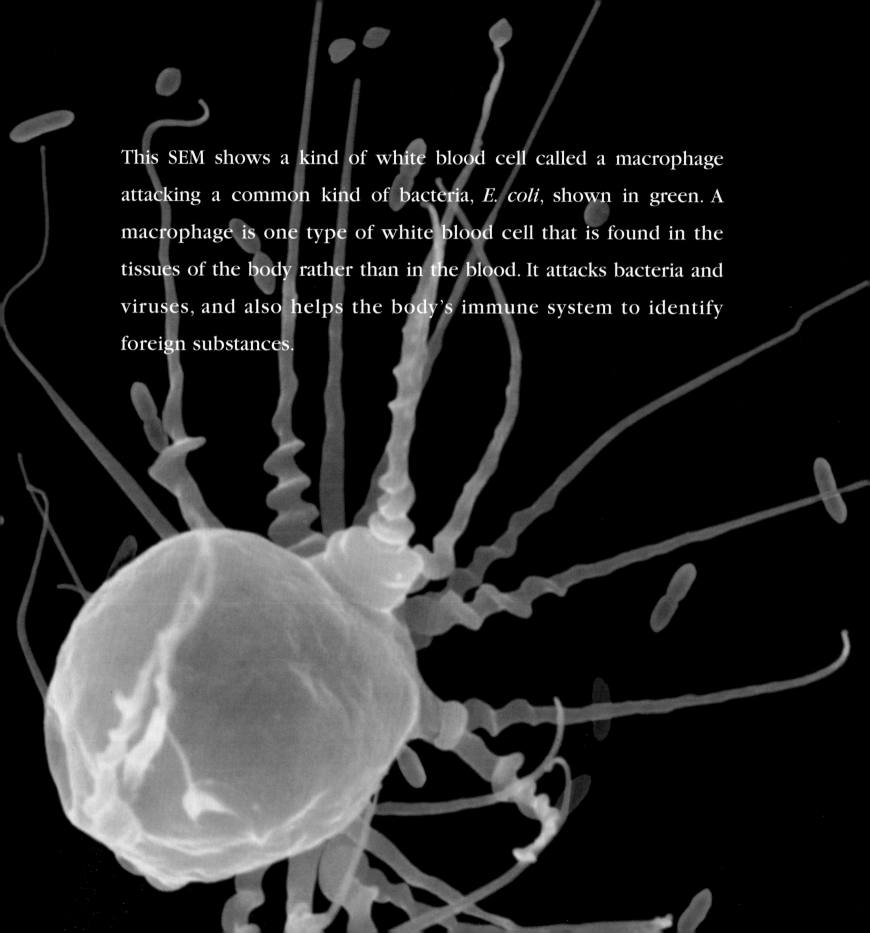

This SEM shows a kind of white blood cell called a macrophage attacking a common kind of bacteria, *E. coli*, shown in green. A macrophage is one type of white blood cell that is found in the tissues of the body rather than in the blood. It attacks bacteria and viruses, and also helps the body's immune system to identify foreign substances.

Hidden Worlds
of Time

Some scientists can catch bullets in flight. No, they're not Superman or Superwoman. They don't use their hands to stop the bullets. Instead they use an electronic flash of light to show us things that happen too fast for the eye to see. The machine they use is called an electronic strobe. It gives off an intense flash of light for one-millionth of a second. Compare that to a wink of an eye, which takes one-fortieth of a second.

Think of one-millionth of a second in this way. Suppose one second was the distance from New York to Los Angeles, about three thousand miles. Then one-millionth of one second would be the distance across a room, about fifteen feet.

Any standard camera can take a split-second photograph using this high-speed flash. This photo of a bullet cutting a playing card in half and the other photographs in this section were taken using strobe techniques first developed by Dr. Harold E. Edgerton more than six decades ago.

The high-speed flash catches the instant impact of a tennis ball on a racket. Notice how the ball is flattened and how the strings of the racket are bent back by the impact. On the next page, the splash of a falling drop of water looks like a crown.

Strobe lights can also be used to make multiple images of moving subjects. Dozens and even hundreds and thousands of photos can be made in a second. These not only show us motion slowed down so that we can understand what is happening, but are beautiful works of art in themselves.

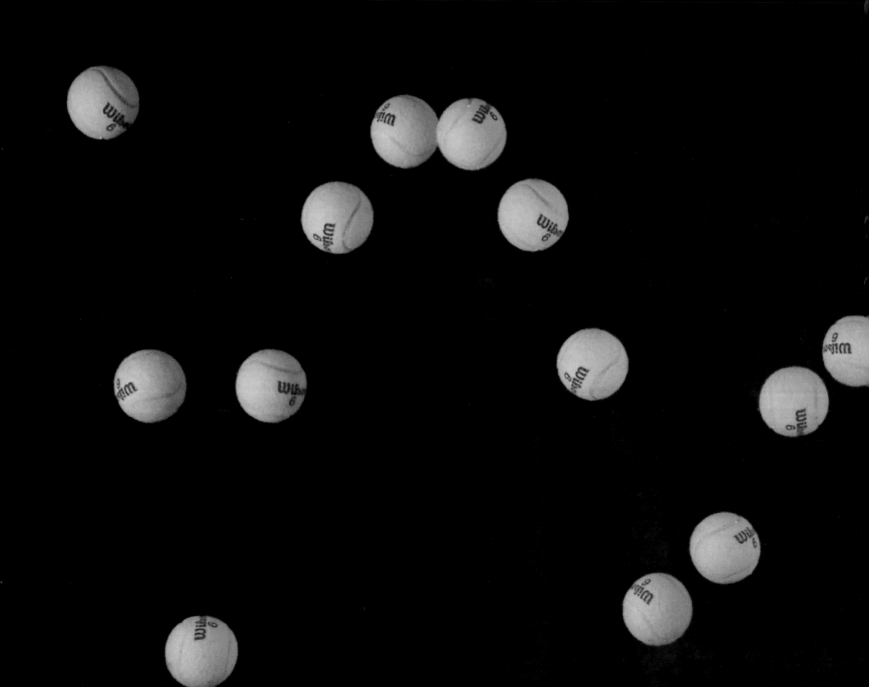

Hidden Worlds of the Earth

Some things are too small for us to see with the human eye; other things are too big for us to see all at once. We can see parts of our planet Earth from the surface, but we can't see all of it except from space. Nowadays, satellite and space probe photos show us our world in many different ways.

This photograph of Hurricane Floyd in the Atlantic Ocean was taken on September 13, 1999, by a weather satellite of the National Oceanic and Atmospheric Administration (NOAA). The colors were added by computer to show wind speeds and directions.

Hurricanes are violent storms that spin out of tropical waters during late summer and early fall. Every minute, a hurricane releases energy equal to several hydrogen bombs. The sustained winds of Hurricane Floyd were nearly 150 miles per hour, an incredibly powerful force that caused great destruction when it hit land.

From space, you can see the "eye" of a hurricane, the dark spot in the center of the photograph, a place of calm winds and sunny skies with the storm raging all around it. The eye of this hurricane was about twenty miles across, while the hurricane itself was 600 miles across.

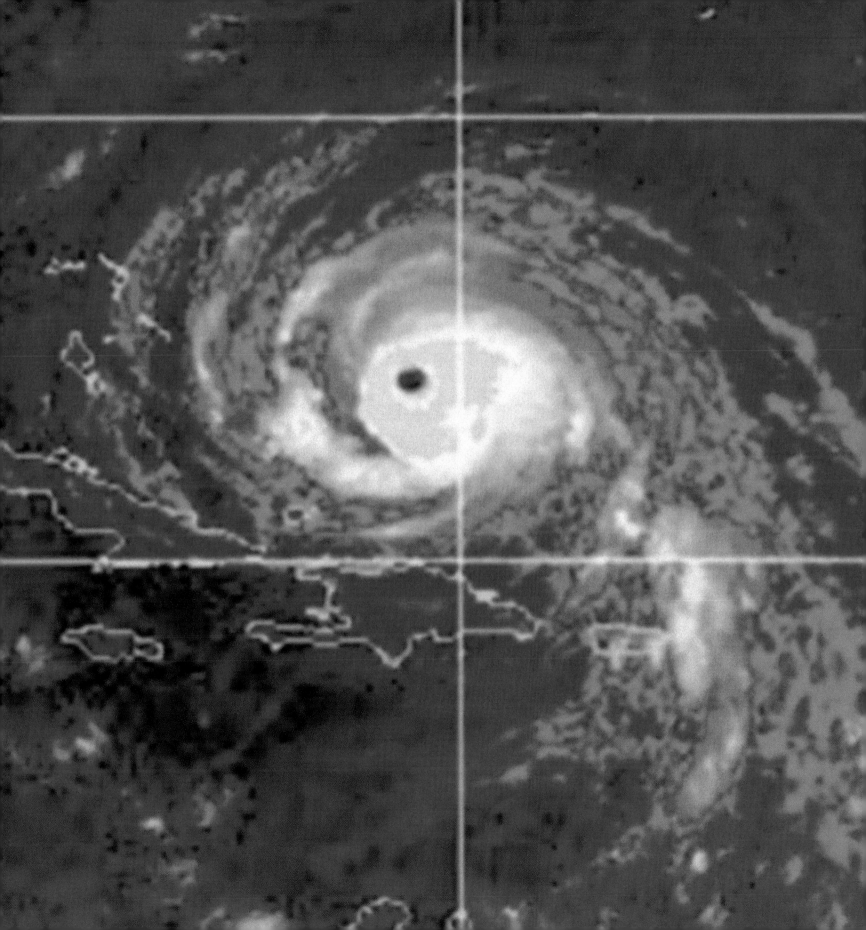

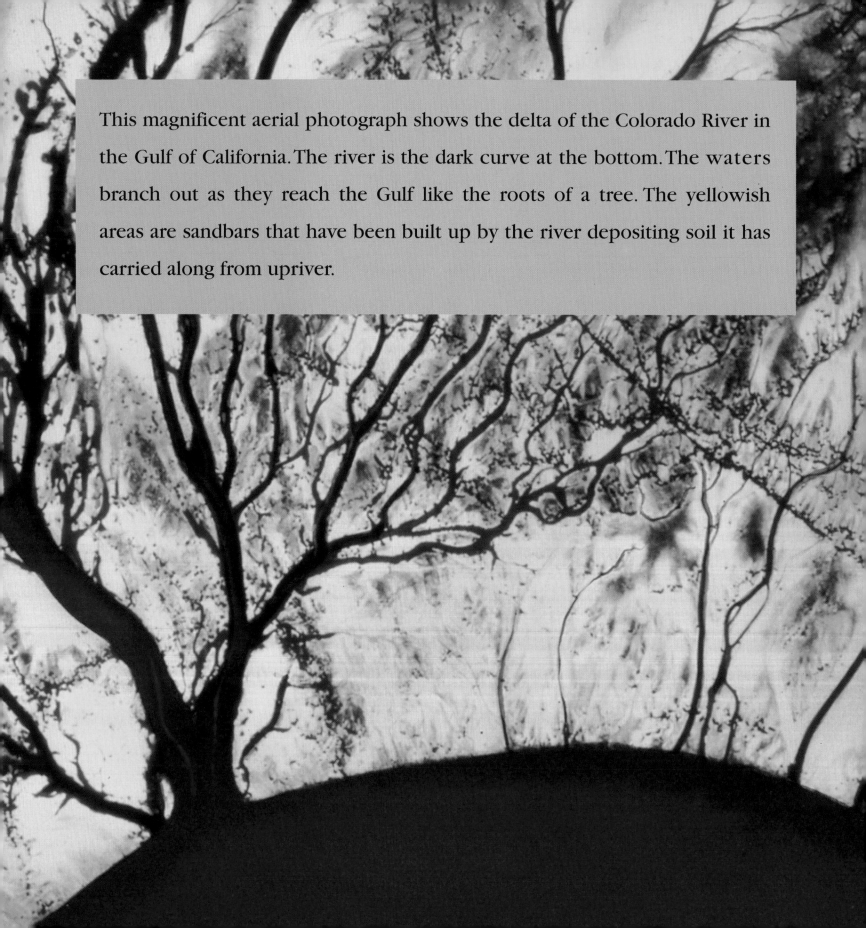

This magnificent aerial photograph shows the delta of the Colorado River in the Gulf of California. The river is the dark curve at the bottom. The waters branch out as they reach the Gulf like the roots of a tree. The yellowish areas are sandbars that have been built up by the river depositing soil it has carried along from upriver.

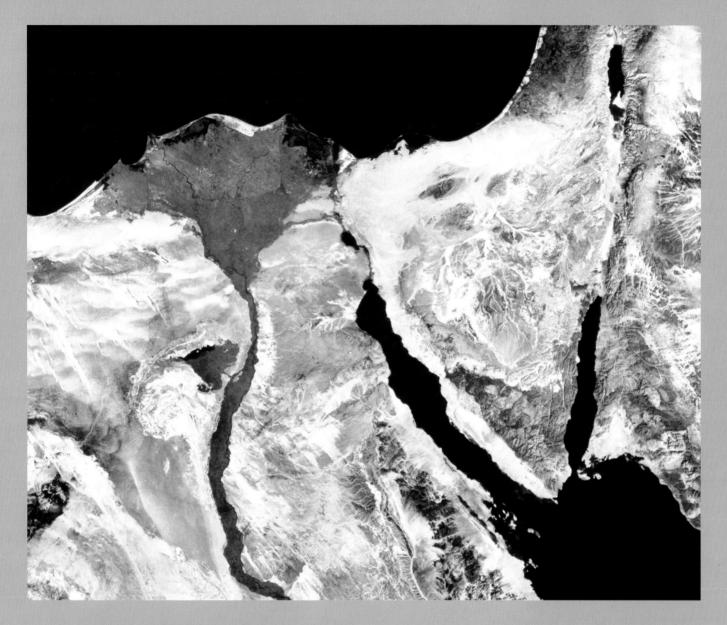

A Landsat satellite, orbiting about 570 miles above Earth, took this infrared photograph. The photograph has been color-enhanced by a computer so that the details can be easily observed. At the left is the Nile River delta, in Egypt. Israel is the land to the upper right. The red color shows agriculture in the fertile delta and in Israel. The city of Cairo is the dark gray area at the base of the delta. Images like this one can tell us much about the effects that humans have upon the land and the environment.

These are sand dunes in the Namibian Desert, seen from a space shuttle. Dunes are hills of loose sand formed in the desert where strong winds tend to blow from one direction. The dunes travel along the ground in the direction the wind is blowing, as much as 100 feet in a year. The dune fields in Namibia are about 100 miles wide and extend more than 1,200 miles along the coast of southwestern Africa.

This is a satellite photo of the Himalayas, taken from 550 miles above the surface. Snow-covered Mt. Everest, at 29,000 feet, is the tallest mountain in the world. In the middle are the foothills of the Himalayas, with many peaks 3,000 to 4,000 feet high. At the bottom are the high plains surrounding the Ganges River of India.

Hidden Worlds of Space

For many centuries, Earth was assumed to be the center of the universe. After Copernicus's theories in the early 1500s, the sun was thought to be the center of the universe. Then scientists discovered that our sun is a star like the thousands of other stars you see in the sky, and that the stars we see are part of a galaxy we call the Milky Way.

All stars, including our sun, are born within nebulae, gigantic clouds of hydrogen gas and dust in outer space. Stars are born in groups or clusters, but most clusters finally drift apart. Stars change in brightness and size during their lives. Our sun is a medium-aged, medium-small yellow star. A young star may be ten thousand times brighter than our sun is now.

The Hubble Space Telescope took this photo of the Eagle Nebula. The Eagle Nebula is a star-forming region of the Milky Way galaxy, about seven thousand light-years away from our solar system. (A light-year is the distance light travels in one year—about 5.8 million million miles.) The new stars are the bright lights inside the fingerlike bulges at the top of the nebula. Each "fingertip" is tens of billions of miles across—more miles across than our entire solar system.

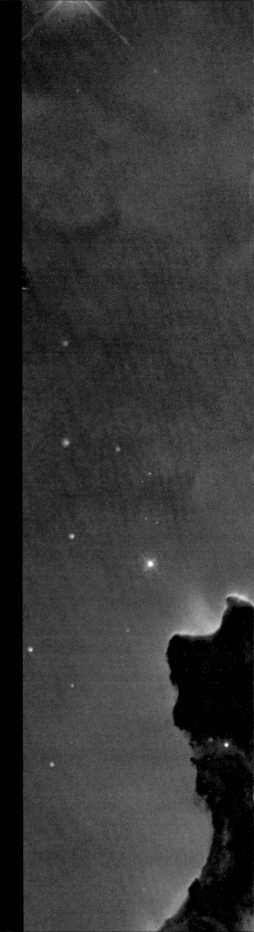

The photograph shows the Great Red Spot on the surface of Jupiter. It was taken from a spacecraft that passed close to the planet and sent back pictures to us by radio waves, much like television. A gigantic superstorm of whirling gases that has already lasted for hundreds of years, the Great Red Spot is more than twice as large as planet Earth.

Like Jupiter, Saturn is made up mostly of gases. Its rings are made of many particles of ice and dust spinning around the planet, some as big as your fingernail, some as big as a house.

This "butterfly" is actually a gigantic nebula in distant space, photographed by the Hubble Space Telescope. Gases are moving 200 miles per second from the central star, like super-supersonic jet engine exhaust. This nebula's size has increased since the star explosion that formed it about 1,200 years ago.

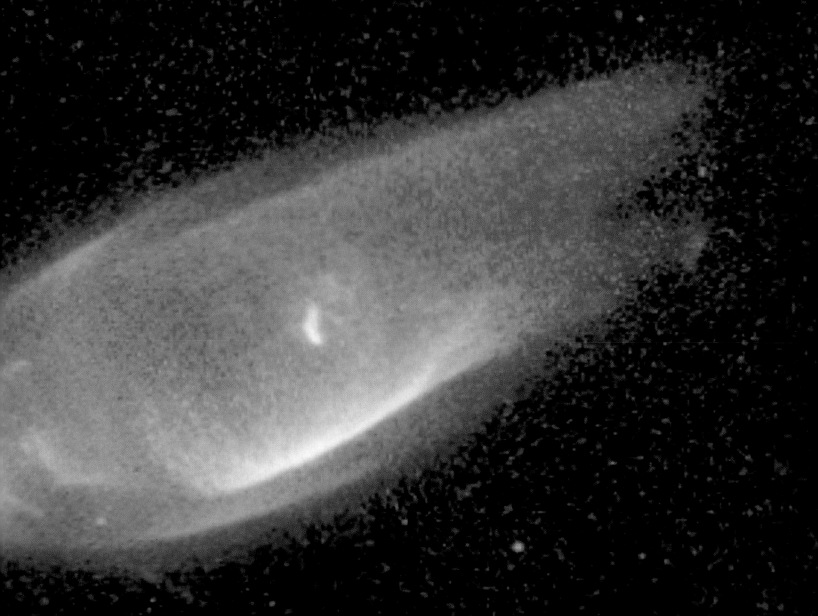

In the past fifty years, many new discoveries have been made in space. Black holes, quasars, pulsars, and supernovas have all become commonplace words. People have landed on the Moon, and a rover has set down on the planet Mars. Space probes, the orbiting Hubble Space Telescope, and other new kinds of instruments help scientists come up with much new information about the planets, the stars, and the galaxies beyond the Milky Way.

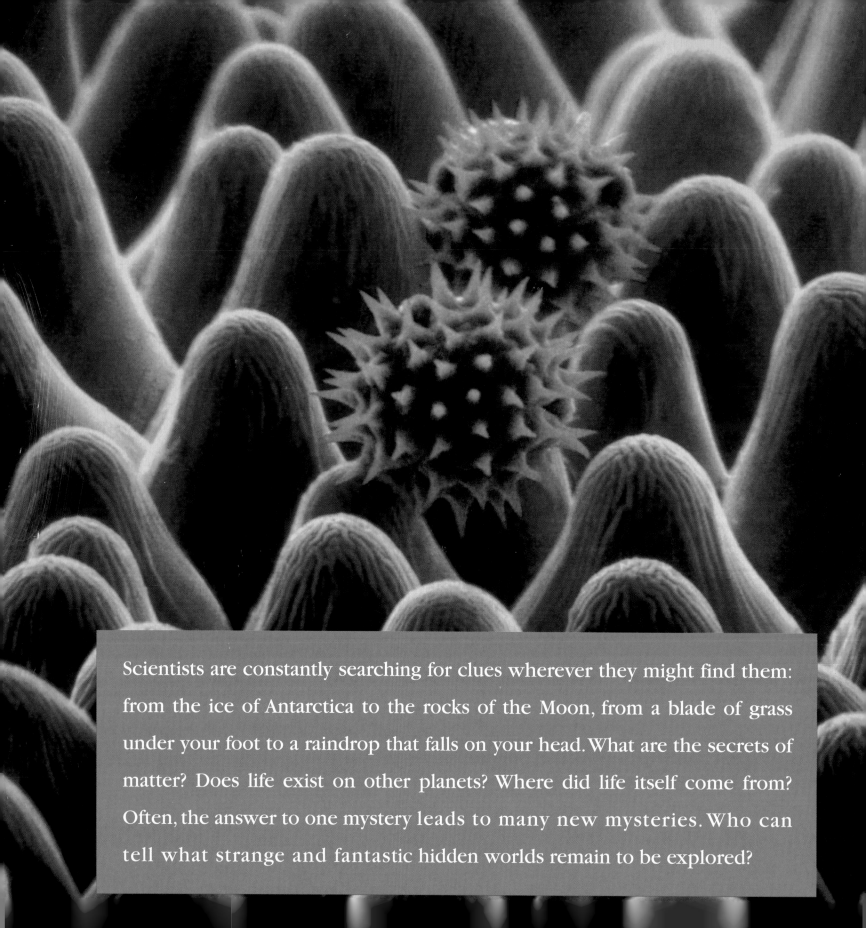

Scientists are constantly searching for clues wherever they might find them: from the ice of Antarctica to the rocks of the Moon, from a blade of grass under your foot to a raindrop that falls on your head. What are the secrets of matter? Does life exist on other planets? Where did life itself come from? Often, the answer to one mystery leads to many new mysteries. Who can tell what strange and fantastic hidden worlds remain to be explored?